ARRANGING FLOWERS
IN A
VASE

JUDITH BLACKLOCK

The Flower Press

Published by
The Flower Press Ltd
3 East Avenue
Bournemouth
BH3 7BW

A CIP catalogue record for this book is available from the British Library.

ISBN-13: 978 0993 571 510

Design: Amanda Hawkes
Cover photograph: Oliver Gordon

Printed and bound in China by C & C Offset Printing Co., Ltd.

Contents

Introduction

I don't know anyone who is not moved by a beautiful display of flowers in a vase … or perhaps I have just been mixing with the right people! In writing this book, my aim is to help everyone, wherever they live and whatever their ability, to have fun creating floral displays that will give great pleasure. You really don't need to spend a lot of money on flowers or on vases. It is possible to make gorgeous arrangements with or without a garden, whether you have a few pounds or a fortune.

But what is a vase? Convention dictates that it is a container specifically for flowers that is usually taller than it is wide. However, with floral fashion now favouring a much looser approach, a vase today can be anything that holds flowers, from the finest antique Wedgwood urn to a baked bean tin, via jugs, bowls, teacups and jam jars – as you will see in this book.

Over the years I have come up with a number of guidelines that are easy to understand. If you lack confidence with flowers, just follow my advice and you won't go wrong. And then, when you are comfortable with your arranging, you can go on to experiment and develop your skills. You will never stop learning, but the route will be

clearer. With the choice of flowers on offer these days, you will certainly never get bored.

Start with my top ten tips (see opposite) and let them set you thinking. Don't worry if you can't source the flowers and foliage used in the designs. Think in terms of shapes and colours and use whatever is available locally. That way you will be creating your own original work and learning from it. I have listed the plant material used – flowers first alphabetically, then foliage, fruit and berries – followed by the height of the vase (H) and the size of the opening (OP), to give you an idea of scale.

I have loved putting *Arranging Flowers in a Vase* together and hope you will get as much enjoyment from arranging flowers once you've read it. The book will explain all you need to know … and if it doesn't, well, get in touch!

JUDITH BLACKLOCK

Botanical and common names

In the main text a flower's common name is given first, followed by its full botanical name or genus in brackets, abbreviated if appropriate. Where the botanical name is the same as the common name, or so near as to be indistinguishable, only the former is listed: for example, *Lavandula* rather than lavender, *Lilium* rather than lily, *Paeonia* rather than peony. The botanical name is always in italics, the common name never in italics. Where the botanical name is better known than the common name it is the former that is used: for example, *Liatris* rather than gayfeather.

By the image of each design you will find a comprehensive list of all the plant material used, with the species and variety given where known.

My top ten tips

You will find floral advice throughout the book, but the list that follows contains what I consider the most important points to help make your arranging pleasurable and successful from the word go. They are easy to understand and work every time.

1 The volumetric relationship between the vase and the flowers is important. When arranging a mass of flowers, the results will always be pleasing if either the flowers or the vase dominates, thus avoiding eye-pull conflict! The proportions 1.5:1 work well. When arranging only a few stems, allow the flowers to be one and a half times the height of the vase, or even a little bit higher.

2 When selecting a vase for a mass of flowers as opposed to two or three stems, choose one that is half the height of the stems. The flowers will have space between them, thus creating greater volume and as a consequence the proportions will adjust automatically to the approximate ratio 1.5:1.

1.5:1 volume of flowers to vase

3   There are three basic flower shapes:

- round, such as sunflower (*Helianthus*) or *Gerbera*
- spray, such as statice (*Limonium*) or spray *Chrysanthemum*
- linear, such as *Delphinium* and *Gladiolus*

Round forms are the most important in floral design as they dominate and hold the eye. Their strength brings together the other elements of the bouquet harmoniously. I always include a round form in designs of mixed flowers. Spray forms have flowers at the end or along secondary stems. These add softness and interest to the round forms. Linear forms have flowers close to and along the stem. They are usually bold and dramatic. They look great in vases with a ring of interesting foliage encircling the flowers low down so as not to hide any of the petals. When mixing your flowers always ensure that you choose at least one type of bloom with this form.

4   Many people make the mistake of buying a vase that is too tall for their flowers. If you are buying only one vase, make it between 20 and 25 cm high. Most bunches of flowers on sale are between 40 and 50 cm and would be perfect in a vase of this height. If you decide to go for a second vase, I would suggest a 15 cm glass cube for designs with a more contemporary look.

5   A vase in a neutral colour, such as grey, always harmonises well with flowers. A matt rather than a shiny texture will enhance rather than detract from the plant material.

Round   Spray   Linear

6   Flowers that are volumetric, such as daffodils (*Narcissus*), glory lilies (*Gloriosa*), Guernsey lilies (*Nerine*), open *Iris* or *Lilium*, look good on their own or positioned higher in the design than other flowers or foliage. They need space around each bloom to show off their beauty.

7   When you get your flowers home remove the bottom 10 per cent of the stems at an angle and place immediately in clean water in a clean vase to which cut flower food has been added. Follow the manufacturer's recipe for mixing with water. Remove any leaves that will be below the rim.

8   The cooler your room the longer your flowers will last, but whatever the temperature some flowers last longer than others. Don't expect *Iris* to last as long as *Lilium*, or lily-of-the-valley (*Convallaria*) to last as long as carnations (*Dianthus*).

9   Used well, foliage is as beautiful as flowers. It can be grown in the garden or in pots, donated by a neighbour or picked in moderation from hedgerows and common places (but always make sure to take only limited amounts where it is growing abundantly) and will add volume and variety to your vase designs. Cut flowers from the garden are lovely but I prefer to see them growing there, so I would recommend buying your flowers. That said, if you have a garden with a lot of flowers and you can cut without leaving unsightly gaps you're very lucky. You could also try growing varieties where cutting encourages more flowers to open, such as the sweet pea (*Lathyrus*).

10 Space between the flowers is free and you can get a bigger design for less if you allow the flowers to breathe.

Volumetric flowers

Selecting the freshest blooms and knowing how to make them last longer will extend the pleasure gained from arranging flowers. But whatever treatment you give, some flowers will remain fresh longer than others. Roses will last better than iris and carnations will last longer than roses. However, all fresh flowers have certain features in common and this will make your choice easier.

1
Getting started

Purchasing flowers

The ephemeral nature of flowers is part of their challenge yet part of their beauty. Everyone wants to buy the freshest blooms, but this is not always easy. Taking into account the points listed below will help you to make the right selection every time, so that you can enjoy your flowers for longer, whichever ones you buy.

- Flowers in season will be stronger, last longer and be less expensive.

- Choose a good source by checking that the retailer's containers holding the flowers have water and are clean.

- Flowers positioned outside a shop or garage are vulnerable to draughts and extreme temperatures, which cause damage and therefore shorten their life.

- The scent of fragrant flowers is stronger in a fresh as opposed to an older flower and in a warmer as opposed to a cooler room.

- Avoid purchasing flowers that have brown marks on their petals. This is probably botrytis, a fungal disease that spreads rapidly. Pale-coloured roses and lisianthus (*Eustoma*) are particularly at risk. If you do not notice the brown marks until arranging, simply remove the affected petals.

- If the petals are translucent or crêpey, the flowers may have been kept too long, or at too low a temperature, in a cold store.

- Many buds that do not show any colour are unlikely to open: think spray carnation (*Dianthus*), *Freesia* and *Paeonia*.

- Fresh flowers have green or grey foliage but not yellow, which is often the sign of an older bloom. The majority of flowers are sold with leaves attached, although there are exceptions, such as *Allium*, amaryllis (*Hippeastrum*), calla (*Zantedeschia*), daffodil (*Narcissus*), *Gerbera* and Guernsey lily (*Nerine*). The leaves of some flowers, such as *Chrysanthemum*, fade first, so removing them gives the impression of a fresher flower.

- Double flowers generally last longer than single flowers.

- If there is pollen on the petals it is an indication that the flower is coming to the end of its life.

- Avoid purchasing disc-petalled flowers, such as spray *Chrysanthemum*, *Dahlia*, *Gerbera* and sunflower (*Helianthus*), with petals missing as others are likely to fall.

- Supermarkets and flower stalls may offer the cheapest flowers but your professional local florist is the person who will be able to advise you best.

- Although all supermarkets have a policy regarding the care of flowers, it is the individuals assigned to the flower department in each store who determine whether they are well looked after or not. Check the water in the bucket, how many flowers have reached the sell-by date (this is an indication of whether they have good stock control) and how fresh they look. Find a supermarket where the person in charge is someone special.

Chicken wire

Chicken wire, sometimes known as wire netting, can be used decoratively or as a hidden mechanic. Purchase with a 5 cm gauge as, when crumpled, the holes in anything smaller will not be big enough to take most stems.

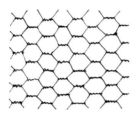

- To use chicken wire in a tall vase cut a length that is twice the height and a little wider than the vase. For a low, wide vase cut a length that is twice the width and only a little taller. Cut off the hard edges, scrunch in the hands and insert in the vase, taking care that it does not scratch delicate surfaces. Ensure that the chicken wire is not all tucked inside the vase but allow some to rise above the rim, so that stems can be angled out of the sides.

- If you have only a small amount of chicken wire you may prefer to wedge it in the neck of the vase and thread the flowers through.

- Decorative metallic chicken wire looks attractive and also gives support for stems. A pin holder positioned at the base of a vase can help to keep the stems secure.

RIGHT Chicken wire is an ideal support for flowers as it keeps the stems in place and allows them to have their ends directly in water.

Plant material: *Celosia argentea* var. *cristata*, spray *Rosa* 'Babe', *Rosa* 'Red Naomi' and *Skimmia japonica* 'Rubella' with *Hypericum* 'Fire Flair' and *Helleborus* foliage

Vase: H 20 cm, OP 10 cm

Floral foam

When you wish to create elaborate or large displays, floral foam can be a useful way of keeping your stems in place. However, it is vital that you soak the foam correctly, otherwise it will be wet on the outside and dry inside, which means that the stems will be unable to draw up water and will die, even if water is added to the vase. To soak foam correctly, place it in still water that is deeper than the piece being soaked. Allow it to sink under its own weight until it is level with the water and the colour has changed from light to dark green. Remove and use.

● If floral foam is placed at the bottom of a vase, it is a useful support for displaying a few stems, particularly if the opening is wide. Conversely, if you are creating a huge design with many stems – for example, in an urn – it is best to cut the foam to rise higher than the rim of the container, so that the stems can be angled in all directions and the flowers and container work as one.

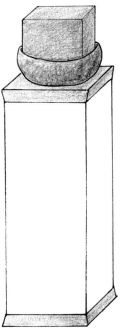

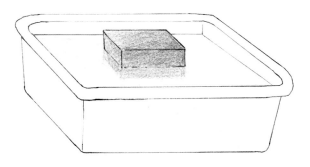

RIGHT This large classic design in a period vase was easier to create than it looks, as foam was used as a means of keeping the stems in place. The foam rose well above the rim of the vase so that stems could be inserted at every angle. Large roses from my garden, in an eclectic mix of colours, were combined with foliage from the redcurrant bush (*Ribes*) and other shrubs that needed pruning in the height of summer.

Plant material: *Astilbe* 'Europa', *Clematis* 'Blue Pirouette', mini *Gerbera* 'Lemon Ice', *Hydrangea*, *Paeonia lactiflora* 'Sarah Bernhardt', *Rosa* (garden), *Scabiosa caucasica*, *Valeriana officinalis* and *Viburnum opulus* 'Roseum' with *Acer palmatum*, *Cotinus coggygria* 'Royal Purple', *Hosta* 'Paul's Glory', *Physocarpus opulifolius* 'Diabolo' and *Ribes sanguineum*

Vase: H 30 cm, OP 17 cm

ABOVE Basket moss (*Sphagnum*) was placed at the bottom of a fishbowl vase and a few short stems of blue spruce (*Picea pungens*) and three *Cymbidium* orchid blooms were inserted through. The addition of a few baubles, in scale with the vase and flowers, creates a festive arrangement that will last for weeks and is ideal for short stems that don't need a huge amount of support.

Plant material: *Cymbidium* 'Yellow River Monica' with *Picea pungens* and *Sphagnum*

Vase: H 18 cm, OP 15 cm

RIGHT Tiny floral gel beads expand when soaked in water for several hours and change into a frog-spawn lookalike that can be used to position your stems. They can be purchased coloured or you can add food dye. I am not the biggest lover of coloured gel beads, but when these were added to this lily vase I found the combination with the lemon *Phalaenopsis* orchids and kentia palm (*Howea*) rather appealing. I rather wish I had added an umbrella to finish the cocktail! Just be aware that gel beads must not be disposed of down domestic drains as blockages are likely to occur.

Plant material: *Phalaenopsis* 'Anthura Detroit' with *Howea* and *Dracaena surculosa*

Vase: H 60 cm, OP 20 cm

LEFTT In this design by Bo Büll, a sliver of foam, covered with sand, has been placed at the bottom of a low glass container. Flowers and grasses have then been inserted in the foam.

Plant material: *Allium nigrum, Antirrhinum, Argyranthemum frutescens, Dianthus* (spray), *Eryngium* 'Sirius Questar' and *Papaver somniferum* with *Briza media* and *Chasmanthium latifolium*

Vase: H 8 cm, OP 25 cm

ABOVE Dutch flower bricks have numerous small openings in the top. Tall stems would look ill at ease, so arrange flowers on short stems. Here a head of *Hydrangea* from the garden has been split into small sprays and inserted through some of the holes to create a low, compact massed design.

Plant material: *Hydrangea*

Vases: behind H 8 cm, OP 15 cm; in front H 4 cm, OP 8 cm

Now that many aspects of the practical side of arranging have been covered, the next chapter focuses on how to maximise the beauty of flowers through an appreciation of the elements and principles of design.

If you follow the criteria outlined in the elements and principles of design you will be able to select flowers and vases that work together harmoniously. These elements and principles can be applied to all the arts: sculpture, textiles and garden design, to name just a few. Once you understand them, your world will be transformed as your analytical side enjoys the challenge of working out why your flowers look so good!

3

The elements
and principles
of design

Elements of design

The four elements describe the plant material that you choose to use. They are:

- form
- colour
- texture
- space

Form

The form or shape of most flowers can be classified as being round, linear or spray. When choosing flowers to work together harmoniously try to include at least one with a round form, such as a carnation (*Dianthus*), *Dahlia*, *Gerbera*, *Paeonia*, open *Rosa* or sunflower (*Helianthus*). Round is always the dominant form in design because it attracts and holds the eye. It works with linear and spray forms to create arrangements that have focus and strength.

In small designs a spray form with limited round flowers, such as spray carnations and lisianthus (*Eustoma*), rather than those with a multitude of flowers, such as baby's breath (*Gypsophila*) and waxflower (*Chamelaucium*), will do the trick, particularly in the loose garden style which is so prevalent at the moment.

When working with form, bear in mind two things. First, flowers of one type are often the easiest to arrange. Second, flowers that are volumetric – that is, have space within – such as daffodils (*Narcissus*), *Gloriosa superba* 'Rothschildiana', *Iris* or *Lilium*, are always easier to arrange on their own or at a higher level than other flowers. I feel they need space around them to show off their beauty.

ABOVE Beautiful open *Anemone* has a round form, which is the strongest in design terms. When selecting an assortment of flowers, always include this form and you will be assured of a pleasing mix.

Plant material: *Anemone coronaria*

Vase: H 15 cm, OP 10 cm

RIGHT With a linear flower, such as *Delphinium*, emphasise the vertical movement and extend the height up to twice that of the vase. Do be sure to remove any flower heads that fall below the rim. Rather than throwing them away, use them to make confetti or potpourri by leaving them to dry on metal trays on a window ledge. In warm weather this will take only a few days.

Plant material: *Delphinium elatum*

Vase: H 34 cm, OP 10 cm

ABOVE Queen Anne's lace (*Anthriscus*) has a spray form, which is delightful when massed in a tall vase. If arranged with other flowers its form can get confused and lose its delicacy and lightness. Filling a vase with only one flower is an easy way to achieve success.

Plant material: *Anthriscus sylvestris*

Vase: H 35 cm, OP 15 cm

RIGHT In this design open *Tulipa* give a round form, throatwort (*Trachelium*) spray and willow (*Salix*) linear. When combined, these three forms complement each other perfectly.

Plant material: *Salix caprea, Trachelium caeruleum* and *Tulipa* 'Foxtrot'

Vase: H 25 cm, OP 14 cm

RIGHT The composition of this extravagant mix of glorious flowers is held together by the bold round shapes of the roses and peonies. The spray forms of lady's mantle (*Alchemilla mollis*), *Bouvardia* and guelder rose (*Viburnum opulus* 'Roseum'), together with fragrant herbs, support by giving contrast and interest, while the linear *Delphinium* takes the electric blue deep into the design.

Plant material: *Alchemilla mollis, Ammi majus, Bouvardia longiflora, Chamelaucium uncinatum, Delphinium elatum, Paeonia lactiflora* 'Sarah Bernhardt', *Rosa* 'Secret Love', *Tulipa* 'Caramba' and *Viburnum opulus* 'Roseum' with *Danae racemosa, Hedera helix, Myrtus communis* and *Rosmarinus officinalis*

Vase: H 18 cm, OP 12 cm

Colour

Studying the colour wheel in depth can seem so complicated. Having taught the theory for many years, I believe it is best to learn just the most basic facts, which can be easily absorbed and understood. Then you can go it alone and pick up the rest through experience. You will soon begin to see why one colour scheme works and another does not.

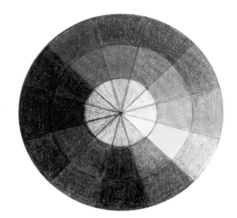

- There are three colours that cannot be created by mixing other colours together: blue, red and yellow. These are called primary colours.

- Secondary colours are created by mixing two of the three primary colours together to create purple (red and blue), orange (red and yellow) and green (blue and yellow).

- Tertiary colours are created by mixing two of the primary and secondary colours together. These are purple-red, purple-blue, orange-red, orange-yellow, blue-green and blue-yellow.

- Primary, secondary and tertiary colours can be dynamic but they are not always restful on the eye. If you add white to one of them the resulting colour (a tint or pastel) is diluted and softer – think pink rather than red. Conversely, the addition of black or grey (black and white) creates a shade or tone and is more subdued.

- Achromatic (literally, without colour) is a term used for very weak colours, perhaps most easily explained as greyed or neutral colour. These are perfect colours for vases.

- Blues and purples are very popular. Together with green, they are cool colours and they are recessive, which means that they recede into the background, making them difficult to see in a large space or in dim lighting. Yellow followed by orange, red, green and then blue and purple is the order for easy visibility.

- Red, orange and yellow are warm colours and are easier to see than the other colours in the wheel. They work harmoniously together.

- Lime green can be added to virtually all colour schemes to give energy, brightness and joy. Think guelder rose (*Viburnum opulus* 'Roseum'), lady's mantle (*Alchemilla mollis*) and green spurge (*Euphorbia esula*).

- Don't try to repeat all the colours of your room with your flowers, just pick out two or three.

- If you have a dark entrance think about using light pastel colours as they are easier to see than dark or recessive colours in a dim light.

Colour schemes

- A monochromatic colour scheme uses one colour only, but this can include tints, tones and shades as well as the full colour. Interest in the arrangement can be heightened by incorporating strong textural contrasts. This is an easy colour scheme to work with.

- An adjacent colour scheme uses up to one-third of the colour wheel, the colours all being found next to each other. In flower arranging it is accepted that green may also be included – this is the flower arranger's neutral colour. An example would be green-yellow, yellow, yellow-orange and orange, plus green. This colour scheme is also a safe option.

- A complementary colour scheme, achieved by combining colours from opposite sides of the colour wheel, such as yellow and purple, is immediately dynamic.

Any two complementary colours used together will intensify and enhance each other brilliantly. For example, combine blue cornflowers (*Centaurea*) with orange *Rosa* and observe the interplay between the two colours. Avoid using equal amounts of the two colours as the eye will not know where to focus when both are equal. At the same time, do not use just one flower of a different colour as it will be too dominant.

- A polychromatic colour scheme uses many colours together and is always vibrant. The use of plain green foliage will bring all the colours together harmoniously.

ABOVE Here a soft-pink container is filled with pale-pink *Chelome*, *Rosa* and deep-pink *Heuchera* leaves to create a monochromatic design based on the colour red.

Plant material: *Chelome obliqua* and *Rosa* 'Ocean Song' with *Heuchera villosa* 'Palace Purple'

Vase: H 9 cm, OP 17 cm

RIGHT Red and green, blue and orange, and yellow and purple are complementary colours – that is, they are opposites on the colour wheel. As the term implies, they show each other off to advantage, as seen here with the green container holding red spray *Chrysanthemum*, which have been inserted in a hemisphere of foam resting on a wired frame constructed from lengths of lichen-covered twigs.

Plant material: *Chrysanthemum* 'Redstart' with lichen-covered twigs

Vase: H 22 cm, OP 15 cm

Space

Space between the flowers is often an indication that the design is in the classic style. Where the plant material is massed tightly together usually, but not always, the design has a more contemporary feel.

- Incorporating space between the flowers can create a larger display with fewer flowers that therefore costs less.

- Enclosed space is dynamic and interesting and is easily created by adding looped grasses or flexible stems over or around the design.

- Always display your flowers with space around so that the beauty of the arrangement can be seen and appreciated.

BELOW Space is essential to all good design work. Here looped willow (*Salix*) creates enclosed space around and within a hand-tied design composed of folded *Aspidistra* leaves, roses and laurustinus (*Viburnum tinus*).

Plant material: *Rosa* 'Deep Water', *Rosa* 'Purple Hazel', *Salix caprea* and *Viburnum tinus* with *Aspidistra*

Vase: H 22 cm, OP 11 cm

RIGHT The graceful flowers and intriguing seed heads of Japanese anemone (*Anemone hupehensis*) are enhanced by space within and around, allowing each part of the arrangement – flowers, stems and seed heads – to be seen and enjoyed.

Plant material: *Anemone hupehensis*

Vase: H 25 cm, OP 4 cm

Principles of design

The six principles are all about taking the elements and using them to create good design. They are:

- balance
- proportion
- scale
- contrast
- dominance
- rhythm

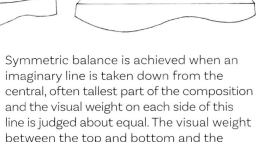

Balance

Balance, which is what underpins all good designs, doesn't just mean that the vase of flowers mustn't fall over; it mustn't look as if it is about to fall over either. There are two types of balance, symmetric and asymmetric, the first of which is much easier to achieve than the second. Fortunately, the vast majority of flowers in a vase call for symmetric balance!

- Symmetric balance is achieved when an imaginary line is taken down from the central, often tallest part of the composition and the visual weight on each side of this line is judged about equal. The visual weight between the top and bottom and the front and back should also be considered.

- Asymmetric balance is when the visual weight is different on each side of the central axis. The vase needs to be balanced by a second arrangement, or an object such as a lamp, to work well.

- Good balance is linked to good proportion. If good proportions are not achieved the arrangement will look top or bottom heavy.

LEFT In this display of late spring flowers the volume of plant material is about one and a half times the volume of the sculptural vase to give classic proportions.

Plant material: *Clematis* 'Star River', *Matthiola* 'Lavender' and spray *Rosa* 'Snowflake'

Vase: H 23 cm, OP 6 cm

RIGHT In this design, blue *Agapanthus* provide a clean, harmonious contrast to the vase. As mentioned on page 61, when you have only a limited number of stems think of proportion 1.5:1 in terms of height, not volume.

Plant material: *Agapanthus* 'Atlantic Ocean'

Vase: H 28 cm, OP 6 cm

ABOVE These two arrangements show how good proportion can be achieved by having either the container about one and a half times the volume of the flowers (on the left) or the flowers one and a half times the volume of the container (on the right). If more flowers were added on the left or taken out on the right, the flowers and vases would have equal proportions with no dominance and as a result the designs would be less pleasing.

Plant material: *Narcissus* 'Jack Snipe' (yellow trumpet) and *Narcissus* 'Romance' (peach trumpet)

Vases: white vase H 30 cm, OP 10 cm; turquoise vase H 18 cm, OP 12 cm

Scale

Scale refers to both the size of one flower in relation to another and the size of the overall arrangement in relation to its surroundings.

- To keep flowers in scale, as a rough guide you should ensure that no flower is more than twice the size of the one next to it.

- Consider the size of your arrangement in relation to the size of the room. A huge design of *Gladiolus* in a small flat would probably not look as good as a simple arrangement of lily-of-the-valley (*Convallaria*) or marigolds (*Tagetes*).

BELOW This tiny Royal Worcester cornucopia, only 8 cm high, holds the flowers from one stem each of spray *Rosa* and sweet William (*Dianthus barbatus*). When arranging flowers in a cornucopia I like to keep the stems short and make a compact mass of blooms rather than imitating the overall form of the vase. The small boxes on the table are also in scale with the size of the arrangement.

Plant material: *Dianthus barbatus* and spray *Rosa* 'Keano'

Vase: H 8 cm, OP 5 cm

ABOVE In this tiny design within a column of glass, the spray *Rosa* and *Eucalyptus* leaves are in harmony with the size of the vase.

Plant material: spray *Rosa* 'Lydia' with *Eucalyptus cinerea*

Vase: H 17 cm, OP 6 cm

RIGHT Huge *Hydrangea*, large painter's palette (*Anthurium*), long arching sprays of berries and branches of preserved oak (*Quercus*) are in scale with each other and with the size of this tall silver vase. Tiny, delicate flowers would not look right in this design.

Plant material: *Anthurium andreanum* 'Calisto' and *Hydrangea* with *Quercus rubra* and *Rosa* hips

Vase: H 120 cm, OP 16 cm

Contrast

Contrast is the difference between objects placed next to each other and it can be obvious or subtle.

- If using more than one type of flower or foliage avoid those that are too similar, as there will be insufficient contrast and the effect will be muddied. Spray baby's breath (*Gypsophila*), golden rod (*Solidago*) and waxflower (*Chamelaucium*) really don't look good together if there is not a round form to provide contrast.

- Strong textural contrasts are needed in designs of one colour or of dried plant material.

- Complementary colours, such as red and green, blue and orange, and yellow and purple, make the strongest contrasts.

- If colour contrasts are gentle, strong form and texture need to be considered.

ABOVE In this simple design of double *Tulipa* and pine (*Pinus*), the straight stems of cherry blossom (*Prunus*) give contrast of form, while the vase gives contrast of texture and colour.

Plant material: *Prunus triloba* and *Tulipa* 'Foxtrot' with *Pinus sylvestris*

Vase: H 18 cm, OP 12 cm

RIGHT The same but different – subtle contrast is evident in this design in matching green vases. Although the plant material is the same, the variation is in how it is positioned.

Plant material: *Ranunculus asiaticus* 'Azur White', *Salix caprea* and *Viburnum opulus* 'Roseum'

Vases: H 34 cm, OP 10 cm

Dominance

If your flowers overpower the vase obviously the arrangement will appear precariously unbalanced. The same applies if the vase is huge in relation to the flowers. The aim is to have sufficient dominance so that there is a sense of order, thus giving unity or harmony.

- A smooth, shiny texture is more dominant than a rough texture.

- Round is the strongest of the three forms and if used in a bouquet of mixed plant material provides dominance.

- Pale tints of a colour are more dominant than darker ones, so if you are using a combination make sure they are in proportion. On the colour wheel yellow is the most dominant colour, followed by orange, red, green and blue, with purple being the least dominant colour.

- The larger the flower the more dominant it will be, all other things being equal.

LEFT In a display of mixed flowers it is the round form that gives dominance, provided here by the pink mini *Gerbera*.

Plant material: *Bupleurum* 'Griffithii', *Chrysanthemum* 'Celtic', *Dianthus barbatus*, double *Eustoma*, mini *Gerbera* 'Kanfetta', *Hypericum* 'Magic Green Power' and *Solidago* 'Carzan Glory' with *Viburnum tinus*

Vase: H 18 cm, OP 13 cm

RIGHT Here the vases are more dominant than the flowers, and this works well because of the brightly patterned wallpaper against which they are displayed.

Plant material: *Alchemilla mollis*, *Dahlia* 'Onesta' and spray *Rosa* 'Lovely Lydia'

Vase: H 15 cm, OP 6 cm

LEFT The dominant flowers here are the cream double *Tulipa* due to their open form, the number of blooms and their advancing colour. The size of the lisianthus (*Eustoma*) is similar but it has recessive purple colouring and is therefore less dominant.

Plant material: *Eustoma russellianum* 'Rosita Blue', *Tulipa* 'Double White' and *Viburnum opulus* 'Roseum' with *Heuchera villosa* 'Palace Purple'

Vase: H 27 cm, O 11 cm

Rhythm

Pleasing rhythm holds the eye in the same way that the beat of pleasing music holds the ear. It can be classic or contemporary. But how is it achieved?

- Good rhythm can be achieved through the radiation of uninterrupted lines that flow from a central point.

- The eye instinctively looks for associations, so repeat colours, forms or textures.

- Rhythm can be created through the placement of a series of mini vases or jam jars along a table or window ledge.

- If your table is round choose a round vase and if it is square go for a cube vase.

RIGHT In this classic design of summer flowers all the stems appear to radiate from a central area, giving a fluid sense of rhythm.

Plant material: *Alchemilla mollis, Dianthus* 'Liberty', *Eustoma russellianum* 'Mariachi Lavender', *Rosa* 'Sweet Dolomiti' and *Scabiosa* 'Lisa' with *Ruscus hypophyllum*

Vase: H 15 cm, OP 13 cm

ABOVE Multiple placements with some form of link always work well, whether arranged in a line, a circle or a zigzag. These three vases are filled with different flowers, but the fact that they are of similar size and material gives a common theme which leads the eye along the design with ease.

Plant material: *Eustoma russellianum* 'Pink Flash' with (from left to right) *Skimmia japonica* 'Rubella', *Muscari* and spray *Rosa* 'Jana'

Vases: shortest H 8 cm, OP 6 cm (two on left); tallest H 10 cm, OP 5 cm (right)

Shape

The wide variety of vase shapes can seem overwhelming. If you don't know where to start, you could do worse than consider a bestselling glass vase sold by IKEA. It may not be wildly inspiring, it may not be suitable for the most cutting-edge designer home, but the cost is seriously low. The opening and the base are about the same in diameter and – guess what – the height is 20 cm, making it perfect for many bunches of flowers.

- Vases that flare at the top and bottom and are about equal in width will always produce good results.

- Tall, straight-sided vases are easier to use if they flare out at the top unless you are working with very straight plant material, such as *Liatris* or *Delphinium*.

- Cylindrical and square vases are easier to fill than those that are letter-box shape or oval. They also look good with fewer flowers.

ABOVE Vases that are wider at the base need flowers that will give volume and width, otherwise the design will appear bottom heavy. The beautiful lime-green *Bupleurum* looks wonderful flowing out of these three different-sized vases.

Plant material: *Bupleurum rotundifolium* 'Griffithii'

Vases: tallest H 31, OP 10 cm; middle H 21 cm, OP 8.5 cm; shortest H 15 cm, OP 5.5 cm

RIGHT This inexpensive 20 cm high glass vase is not the most glamorous of containers but the flare at the top and bottom makes it easy to use. This long-lasting design has been created using a mix of foliage and 20 stems of one type of flower, in this case *Anemone*.

Plant material: *Anemone coronaria* with *Choisya ternata* 'Sundance' and *Cordyline fruticosa* 'Compacta'

Vase: H 20 cm, OP 12 cm

BELOW Letter-box vases are tricky: if there are too few flowers, the stems fall to the outside edges, so you need a lot! Alternatively, try a vertical design using a sliver of foam at the base to help keep the stems in place. Here twigs were placed in position first, followed by a few stems of daffodils (*Narcissus*) and blue grape hyacinths (*Muscari*), with their ends in tubes to avoid contact with the toxic daffodils.

Plant material: *Muscari armeniacum* and *Narcissus* 'Pistachio' with *Betula*

Vase: H 14 cm, OP 28 cm

RIGHT A rectangular vase can hold a lot of plant material – more than you may think or wish for! Here the plant material is divided into two sections. The base is a mass of lime-green guelder rose (*Viburnum opulus* 'Roseum') and the top a pleasing combination of *Veronica* and blue *Clematis*, which gives undulating movement.

Plant material: *Clematis* 'Blue Pirouette', *Veronica* x *media* 'Clea June' and *Viburnum opulus* 'Roseum'

Vase: H 30 cm, OP 15 cm

ABOVE This mix of spring and summer flowers has been arranged in a casual, straight-from-the-garden British style in a greyed terracotta pot that flares at the top and bottom with a wider opening at the top.

Plant material: *Muscari, Myosotis* and *Rosa* (variety unknown) with *Pittosporum tenuifolium*

Vase: H 15.5 cm, OP 17 cm

Colour and pattern

Colour and pattern are important in selecting a vase. A neutral colour is safe and easy, but if you decide to buy a patterned vase don't try to repeat all the colours with flowers. Just choose one or two, so that your arrangement does not look contrived. Here are some general tips.

- Neutral-coloured vases are easy to work with. If buying only one vase, go for a textured grey colour.

- White containers are difficult to link with flowers unless white flowers are included.

- Pewter and tin vases harmonise with pink, pale-blue, cream and white flowers.

- If you always buy the same flowers – say, white *Lilium*, pink roses or orange *Gerbera* – then consider using vases in different colours to create an exciting effect.

RIGHT This blue-lilac vase is partnered with purple lisianthus (*Eustoma*) of a deeper tone, which links with the vase beautifully.

Plant material: *Eustoma russellianum* 'Alissa Blue' and *Eustoma russellianum* 'Rosita Blue'

Vase: H 27 cm, OP 11 cm

RIGHT Blue and yellow work beautifully together and the blue *Iris* with their yellow throats complement this vase perfectly.

Plant material: *Iris* x *hollandica*

Vase: H 23 cm, OP 12 cm

RIGHT White has a visual dominance, especially when the texture is glossy and shiny. If the flowers in a vase like this are strongly coloured there would be too much contrast. Here the mix of white and pastel-coloured flowers creates a harmonious balance that complements rather than distracts.

Plant material: *Chamelaucium uncinatum, Eryngium* 'Supernova Questar', spray *Rosa* 'Jana' and *Rosa* 'Norma Jean' with *Danae racemosa, Rosmarinus officinalis* and *Thlaspi* 'Green Bell'

Vase: H 25 cm, OP 15 cm

Choosing a vase

RIGHT The grey *Eucalyptus* and pale-blue *Hydrangea* are in harmony with the crackled glaze of the silver vase.

Plant material: *Hydrangea* 'Peppermint' with *Eucalyptus pulverulenta* 'Baby Blue'

Vase: H 15 cm, OP 13 cm

Material

Material is a word I deliberated over, but I couldn't think of a better alternative. Whatever your vase is made of, the most important point to check is that it's waterproof before you place it on wood, marble or any other surface that could sustain water damage. You can always place a mat or charger underneath or line the vase with thin plastic film.

- Matt vases with a textured surface are generally easier to work with than those with a smooth, shiny texture, unless you are making a feature of the vase.

- Copper and brass vases suit warmer, richer colours, such as orange, gold, red and purple.

- Silver and pewter vases suit white, cream, pale-blue, pink and lemon-yellow flowers.

- Glass can go misty if washed in the dishwasher on a regular basis. Damage can also occur if the vase is placed upside down in the dishwasher, as the movement of the machine can cause the vase to bounce.

- Delicate flowers, such as lily-of-the-valley (*Convallaria*) and snowdrops (*Galanthus*), need light, delicate vases made of glass or porcelain. More robust flowers, such as *Dahlia*, marigolds (*Tagetes*) and sunflowers (*Helianthus*), work well with heavier, coloured terracotta or pottery vases.

RIGHT The form and visual weight of this vase are perfect for an exuberant mix of flowers against a backdrop of *Eucalyptus* and feathery *Asparagus* fern.

Plant material: *Anthriscus sylvestris, Paeonia lactiflora* 'Sarah Bernhardt', spray *Rosa* 'Romantic Bubbles', *Rosa* 'Upper Secret' and *Tulipa* (French) with *Asparagus setaceus* and *Eucalyptus cinerea*

Vase: H 30 cm, OP 15 cm

LEFT The tints and tones of an autumnal mix of garden and florist's flowers are shown to advantage in a burnished copper jug. The copper tray adds visual weight to the lower part of the design and improves proportion. Foliage from the redcurrant bush and peony have created the initial outline. Foliage from all members of the *Ribes* family is useful once mature and prunings can be incorporated into flower designs after fruiting.

Plant material: *Cosmos*, *Dianthus* 'Dark Farida', *Pelargonium*, spray *Rosa*, *Rosa* 'High & Magic' and *R.* 'Lianne' with *Viburnum opulus* 'Compactum', *Paeonia lactiflora* foliage and *Ribes sanguineum*

Vase: H 22 cm, OP 7 cm

ABOVE A tin watering can is not the easiest container because of its asymmetric shape. Here sweet William (*Dianthus barbatus*) is tightly grouped, low down, so that the mass of blooms is balanced with the spout and handle. The symmetrically arranged mass of *Tulipa*, in a coordinated tin container, creates another part of the overall design.

Plant material: *Dianthus barbatus* and *Tulipa* 'Milka'

Choosing a vase

RIGHT The peach-pink tints of the double lisianthus (*Eustoma*) enhance and reflect the aluminium and copper vases. The blue of the *Delphinium* harmonises with all colours.

Plant material: *Delphinium elatum* 'Blue Bee' and *Eustoma russellianum* 'Arena Champagne'

Vases: H 20 cm, OP 4 cm

Choosing a vase

BELOW Lily-of-the-valley (*Convallaria*), one of the sweetest and most highly desired flowers, will always be expensive to buy due to its delicacy and short life. Its fragrance is delicious. This gentle bloom looks lovely in glass or fine china rather than metal or terracotta.

Plant material: *Convallaria majalis*

Vase: H 10 cm, OP 5 cm

RIGHT This hewn wood has been treated inside to make it waterproof. If the wood hadn't been treated, it would have been easy to place a second container inside. The dominant form, colour and size of the sunflowers (*Helianthus*) make this strong and earthy vase the perfect partner. The colour and pattern of the tablecloth complete the picture.

Plant material: *Helianthus annuus*

Vase: H 22 cm, OP 12 cm

BELOW The sap of daffodils (*Narcissus*) is harmful to the life of other flowers. On their own they are lovely, but if you want an interesting mix try putting them in a vase with a trim of toxin-resilient box (*Buxus*) and then place in a low bowl filled with lemons for an exciting colour match.

Plant material: *Narcissus* 'King Alfred' with *Buxus sempervirens* and *Citrus limon*

Vases: outer H 10 cm, OP 34 cm; inner H 13 cm, OP 12 cm

RIGHT The stems of exotic plant material need a strong, heavy vase so there is no danger of it toppling over. Red ginger (*Alpinia*), *Heliconia* and pigface gourds (*Solanum*) have rigid straight stems and look best in vases with straight rather than curved sides. This vase was perfect, but the stems were too short to give good proportions so I scrunched up cellophane and placed it at the bottom of the vase to raise them.

Plant material: *Alpinia purpurata* and *Heliconia* with *Cordyline fruticosa, Dracaena deremensis, Dracaena fragrans* 'Massangeana', *Microsorum punctatum, Pandanus tectorius* and *Solanum mammosum*

Vase: H 27 cm, OP 17 cm

RIGHT Here I used two containers the same shape but one smaller than the other and lined the space between the two with cinnamon sticks. The inside of the inner vase was filled with foam before the plant material was added. Here I have combined the mini *Gerbera* and deciduous holly (*Ilex*) on a base of *Skimmia japonica* and then incorporated baubles and orange slices. The design was completed with a ribbon tie secured in place with glue dots.

Plant material: mini *Gerbera* 'Wakita' with *Ilex verticillata* and *Skimmia japonica*

Vase: H 15 cm, OP 15 cm

Tricks and tips

BELOW Try placing a few small vases within a larger one. The arrangement will be easier to move and when you add water any drips will be contained. Shasta daisies (*Leucanthemum*) are so easy to grow in the herbaceous border and is also an inexpensive buy from the florist. It lasts incredibly well.

Plant material: *Leucanthemum x superbum*

Vases: outer H 5 cm, OP 20 cm; inner H 7 cm, OP 5 cm

RIGHT Bulb flowers such as *Hyacinthus* often have soil between the leaves which can make the water dirty and look unattractive if they are in a glass vase. Taking ribbon round the vase, in a colour that links with the flowers, hides any debris and all you need is a couple of blobs of florist's fix, Blu-tack or glue dots to keep it in place. A circle of *Anemone*, resting their heads on the rim, completes the design.

Plant material: *Anemone coronaria* and *Hyacinthus*

Vase: H 15 cm, OP 15 cm

ABOVE To distract attention from stems that are not very attractive, insert some that are more interesting, such as colourful, smooth-textured *Cornus* or *Kerria*, into a sliver of foam at the base of the vase and then thread your flowers through.

Plant material: *Rosa* 'Sweet Dolomiti' with *Cornus sericea* 'Flaviramea'

Vase: H 19, OP 17 cm

RIGHT A terracotta pot can be whitewashed or painted to give it a new lease of life.

Plant material: *Hydrangea arborescens* 'Annabelle', *Hypericum* 'Magical Ivory', *Rosa* 'Akito' and spray *Rosa* 'Jana' with *Eucalyptus cinerea*, *Mentha* and *Physocarpus opulifolius* 'Diabolo'

Vase: H 20 cm, OP 20 cm

Tricks and tips

BELOW *Hosta* leaves come in a vast array of colours, shapes and sizes. All of them are a great asset when you need smooth-textured leaves to insert at the base of a vase to hide unattractive stems, give visual weight at the base and/or make a design appear much bigger. Other leaves, such as *Bergenia* and *Aspidistra*, can create a similar effect.

Plant material: *Achillea filipendulina* and *Rosa* 'Crème de la Crème' with *Hosta* 'Paul's Glory' and *Panicum* 'Fountain'

Vase: H 22 cm, OP 12 cm

ABOVE Vibrant mini *Gerbera*, arranged with *Cordyline*, deciduous holly (*Ilex*) and salal (*Gaultheria*) sprayed with a touch of gold, are enhanced with a sumptuous wired bow held in place by a length of stub wire with the ends tucked into the vase. This is an ideal way to hide knobbly or unattractive stems.

Plant material: mini *Gerbera* 'Black Night' with *Cordyline fruticosa*, *Gaultheria shallon* and *Ilex verticillata*

Vase: H 28 cm, OP 13 cm

RIGHT These magnificent *Alstroemeria* were too tall for the vase I wished to use. Rather than chop them down I added *Cordyline* leaves around the flowers to falsely extend the height of the vase. This succeeds in taking the eye smoothly up the design and making the proportions work. Without the *Cordyline* the bouquet would appear top heavy and therefore unbalanced.

Plant material: *Alstroemeria* 'Cape Town' and *Alstroemeria* 'Lemon' with *Cordyline fruticosa*

Vase: H 30 cm, OP 15 cm

Tricks and tips

BELOW Another way to extend the height of the vase is to wedge a plastic bowl, covered in leaves or sympathetic fabric, in the top of the vase. Here a mass of plant material gives contemporary proportions, where the vase is more dominant than the flowers.

Plant material: *Alchemilla mollis, Dianthus barbatus, Eryngium* 'Sirius Questar' and *Rosa* 'White Naomi' with *Cocculus laurifolius* (around the bowl), *Galax urceolata* and *Ruscus hypophyllum*

Vase: H 16 cm, OP 16 cm

Bowl: H 8 cm, OP 18 cm

RIGHT Two heads of bloom *Chrysanthemum* can make a delightful summer design when there is an appealing link between the colour of the flowers and that of the vase. Burgundy *Galax* leaves provide contrast between the two main elements of the design.

Plant material: *Chrysanthemum* 'Anastasia Green' with *Galax urceolata*

Vase: H 12 cm, OP 10 cm

ABOVE *Paeonia* is a much-loved flower and there are never enough blooms in the garden. Here just three single blooms show how easily a pleasing display can be created without huge expense. In this design lengths of thin bark have been wrapped round three jam jars and secured with garden twine.

Plant material: *Paeonia lactiflora* 'Sarah Bernhardt' with *Heuchera villosa* 'Palace Purple'

Vases: H 12 cm, OP 4 cm

RIGHT A Royal Copenhagen vase, filled with globe thistle (*Echinops*) and aromatic mint (*Mentha*), is perfect for the afternoon tea table. Mint spreads profusely in just about any situation or climate and lasts an incredibly long time if placed in water immediately after cutting when it is in season.

Plant material: *Echinops ritro* with *Mentha*

Vase: H 10 cm, OP 3.5 cm

RIGHT Shasta daisies (*Leucanthemum*) from the side of the road and snowberries (*Symphoricarpos*) fill three mini turquoise vases purchased from a craft fair.

Plant material: *Leucanthemum vulgare* with *Symphoricarpos albus*

Vases: H 7 cm, OP 3 cm

LEFT A simple blue vase holds a single stem of *Hydrangea*. The colours are not a perfect match but the frill of meadowsweet (*Filipendula ulmaria*) leaves distracts from any variance and provides harmony. The tiny flowers at the centre of each individual bloom are open which means the *Hydrangea* is more likely to last when cut as it is more mature.

Plant material: *Hydrangea* with *Filipendula ulmaria*

Vase: H 15 cm, OP 8 cm

RIGHT You can't get cheaper than this! The single heads from one stem of spray *Chrysanthemum* have been placed in wine glasses on a silver tray. Tea lights and a single festive bauble were added to complete the picture.

Plant material: spray *Chrysanthemum* 'Bacardi'

Vases: H 14 cm, OP 8 cm

ABOVE One of the few things I have that belonged to my grandmother is a set of coffee cups and these hold a lot of important memories. Here I have filled one with common daisies (*Bellis perennis*), *Lobelia* and pansies (*Viola*) from the garden. The colour and the choice of old-fashioned flowers reinforce the vintage look.

Plant material: *Bellis perennis, Lobelia* and *Viola tricolor*

Vase: H 6 cm, OP 5 cm

RIGHT A pottery vase purchased on a holiday in the south of France was filled with the four o'clock flower (*Mirabilis jalapa*), so called because it opens from late afternoon onwards, wild *Phlox* and berried ivy (*Hedera helix*), all of which were found growing wild locally.

Plant material: *Mirabilis jalapa* and *Phlox paniculata* with *Hedera helix* 'Arborescens'

Vase: H 18 cm, OP 10 cm

Flowers on a budget

RIGHT Vases that are wider at the top than the bottom require a lot of plant material so that the stems can support each other. This vase is filled with a base of *Bupleurum* and green *Hypericum*, with a few stems of spray *Chrysanthemum* and forget-me-not (*Myosotis*) slipped through the network of stems.

Plant material: *Bupleurum*, spray *Chrysanthemum*, *Hypericum* and *Myosotis*

Vase: H 14 cm, OP 20 cm

LEFT I enjoy having flowers growing in my garden and am careful not to take too many for the house. This design shows how you can use just one of this and one of that, perhaps with the addition of some flowers from the florist. Cut them all short, mass in a glass cube filled with clean water and enjoy every bloom.

Plant material: from the garden *Carthamus tinctorius*, *Crocosmia* x *crocosmiiflora* 'Golden Glory', *Dahlia* 'Arabian Night' and *Pelargonium*; from the florist *Chrysanthemum* 'Anastasia' and *Gloriosa superba* 'Rothschildiana'

Vase: H 11 cm, OP 11 cm

BELOW Leaves from strawberry plants (*Fragaria*) are evergreen in my garden and last well when cut. Here I used them as the base for this arrangement in a terracotta vase and then added *Ranunculus* and guelder rose (*Viburnum opulus* 'Roseum') cut short.

Plant material: *Ranunculus asiaticus* 'Elegance Cerise Pink' and *Viburnum opulus* 'Roseum' with *Fragaria* and *Heuchera villosa* 'Palace Purple'

Vase: H 10 cm, OP 15 cm

A huge number of flowers will always look good. However, the skill of making a few blooms look splendid at little or no cost is the real art of the flower designer. I hope this chapter has provided inspiration. Now we look at seasonal flowers.

Although many flowers are now available 12 months of the year, it is lovely to work with flowers that are only around for a short time and hard to source at others. It makes them feel extra special. In Europe we have spring, summer, autumn and winter, but in other parts of the world this is not always the case. I hope readers living in countries that do not have four seasons will find inspiration in these ideas and adapt them to the flowers that are easy to source where they live.

7

Flowers
by season

Spring flowers

- Many spring flowers grow from bulbs and corms. These flowers put on a lot of growth rapidly, which means that their stems are relatively soft compared to the woody stem of a rose. They prefer shallow water that is regularly topped up so their soft stems do not get waterlogged and rot. Because the stems are soft they are not happy if placed in foam.

- The genus *Narcissus*, which includes the daffodil, should not be mixed with other flowers as its sap will shorten their life. If you really want to mix *Narcissus* with other flowers, first place them in water by themselves for several hours and then wipe the stem ends with paper towels before placing with other flowers. Alternatively, use the special cut flower food intended for *Narcissus*. It is said that *Hyacinthus* creates the same problem.

- Shrubby branches of lilac (*Syringa*) and guelder rose (*Viburnum opulus* 'Roseum') will last longer if all the leaves are removed, as these compete with the flowers for water. If purchasing you will be given a special cut flower food for woody stems. Do use this – it really does work!

- The soft stems of spring flowers enjoy breathing space, so don't cram them into a vase but leave space between them.

- Many spring flowers, such as *Ranunculus*, should have all the foliage removed from the stems before arranging as this will lengthen the life of the flowers.

- Most foliage that appears in the early part of the year will be soft and not last when cut, so combine your flowers with evergreen foliage. Alternatively submerge the young leaves under water for half an hour before adding to your flowers – it could help.

LEFT The three vases holding *Anemone*, *Ranunculus* and sprays of lime-green *Bupleurum* have different shapes and sizes but are linked by texture and colour. The placement of similar flowers in these vases creates greater harmony between the three placements.

Plant material: *Anemone coronaria*, *Bupleurum rotundifolium* 'Griffithii', *Ranunculus asiaticus* 'Elegance Yellow', 'Success Lambada', 'Success Omega' and 'Success Rosado'

Vases: tallest H 16 cm, OP 10 cm; middle H 14 cm, OP 9 cm; shortest H 11 cm, OP 8 cm

Flowering cherry (*Prunus*) is delightful in the spring. Take care not to cut it too early, as it will go into leaf rather than producing blossom. In this design three branches have been placed in a line, in floral foam, with a mass of double *Tulipa* cut short and positioned at the base. Tufts of Scot's pine fill in the gaps without distracting from the two major players.

Plant material: *Prunus glandulosa* and *Tulipa* 'Foxtrot' with *Pinus sylvestris*

Vase: H 16 cm, OP 25 cm

This charming multi-patterned jug would be happy with a mix of flowers in the same colour or as shown here with a mass of one type of flower in different colours. Mixed flowers in different colours could be too confusing to the eye and fight with the pattern of the vase.

Plant material: *Hyacinthus orientalis*

Vase: H 16 cm, OP 10 cm

ABOVE This straight-sided glass vase, with a ribbon-look concrete base, holds a mass of daffodils (*Narcissus*) with heads nodding over the rim. The green stems behind the glass form part of the design. A swirl of grape hyacinths (*Muscari*) around the base gives additional interest.

Plant material: *Muscari armeniacum* and *Narcissus* 'Quail'

Vase: H 22 cm, OP 11 cm

LEFT Mimosa (*Acacia*) grows extremely well in the British garden if it is not located in a frost pocket. It flowers early in the spring and produces an abundance of beautiful yellow flowers. It can also be purchased from the florist and gives a bright golden glow on a cold day. A mass looks lovely on its own or you could add yellow *Gerbera* or *Rosa*, as their round form would give interesting contrast.

Plant material: *Acacia dealbata*

Vase: H 30 cm, OP 14 cm

ABOVE A low vintage vase is perfect for the juxtapositioning of spring flowers, all of which are so happy to have their stem ends in water.

Plant material: *Helleborus argutifolius* (green), *Helleborus* x *hybridus*, *Primula vulgaris*, *Vinca major* and *Viola* x *wittrockiana*

Vase: H 4 cm, OP 4 cm

RIGHT *Helleborus* has long been enjoyed as a cut flower from the garden but in recent years it has also been sold commercially. In this design it has been arranged in a 1930s vase, the pattern of which provides subtle additional interest.

Plant material: *Helleborus* x *hybridus*

Vase: H 20 cm, OP 9 cm

ABOVE The colour and bold form of this mass of parrot *Tulipa* complement the round earthenware vase perfectly. *Dracaena* is a long-lasting, strap-like foliage which gives movement and interest when added to flowers in a vase.

Plant material: *Tulipa* 'Libretto' with *Dracaena deremensis*

Vase: H 20 cm, OP 10 cm

RIGHT Lichen-covered twigs have been placed round a straight-sided vase with double-sided tape – a good way to disguise a chipped vase! A rubber band, covered with decorative raffia, has been taken over the twigs to help keep them in place. Foam inside the tin holds an eclectic mix of spring flowers.

Plant material: *Bergenia cordifolia*, *Chaenomeles japonica*, *Helleborus orientalis*, *Muscari armeniacum*, *Ranunculus asiaticus* 'Success Rosado', *Viburnum opulus* 'Roseum' and *Viburnum tinus* with *Arum italicum* subsp. *italicum* 'Marmoratum' and *Heuchera villosa* 'Palace Purple'

Vase: H 15 cm, OP 15 cm

Summer flowers

- Fragrant herbs are at their best from midsummer onwards and can be very long-lasting. Consider *Geranium* leaves, *Lavandula*, marjoram (*Origanum*) and mint (*Mentha*).

- If you like using herbs in your arrangements, purchase a pot from the supermarket. Divide into four and place each one into a pot the same size as the original. Harden off once the weather is clement and you now have four for the price of one.

- Linear flowers, such as *Delphinium*, foxgloves (*Digitalis*), and *Gladiolus*, are gorgeous if cut from the garden because they are straight. However, if purchased from the florist the tips may have become bent by turning to reach the light while packed in boxes. It is impossible to correct this, so either enjoy the stems as they are or trim the tops. It is virtually unknown for these top flowers to open in any event! Growers are now selling these flowers with the tips encased in nylon slip covers to help them remain straight.

- From July, *Hydrangea* comes into season. Only now can they be purchased with confidence. Touch the heads to check if they are firm to the touch, as this is an indication that they will last. Another tip is that if the tiny flowers at the centre of each floret are open there is more chance of the flower lasting.

- Poppy (*Papaver*) seed heads are easy to grow from seed and can be added fresh or dried to vase arrangements. If using dried seed heads with fresh flowers, wrap florist's tape or adhesive tape around the stem ends so that the stems do not go soggy in water.

RIGHT A ring of mini bananas (*Musa*) was wired into a circle and then placed on the rim of the vase. The cross-wires also helped support a mass of beautiful pink *Dahlia* and green sweet William (*Dianthus barbatus* 'Green Trick').

Plant material: *Dahlia* 'Onesta' and *Dianthus barbatus* 'Green Trick' with *Musa*

Vase: H 22 cm, OP 16 cm

ABOVE A sweet-scented garden rose is one of my favourite flowers. They don't last long once cut but every one is treasured. A trio of glass bottles holds these few stems and one or three would be perfect for a summer picnic. The colour of the weather-worn table and drystone wall complements the unstructured form of the pale-pink roses.

Plant material: *Rosa* (variety unknown)

Vases: H 14, 16 and 17 cm, OP 2 cm

LEFT Early summer heralds the gorgeous *Paeonia*. Here *Paeonia lactiflora* 'Sarah Bernhardt' is arranged in a whitewashed earthenware vase with *Astrantia*, lady's mantle (*Alchemilla mollis*) and *Rosa* 'Heaven'. When purchasing *Paeonia* check that colour is showing in the bud or it will not open.

Plant material: *Alchemilla mollis*, *Astrantia major* 'Ruby Star', *Paeonia lactiflora* 'Sarah Bernhardt' and *Rosa* 'Heaven' with *Ruscus hypophyllum*

Vase: H 20 cm, OP 12 cm

Flowers by season

RIGHT A contemporary painting is complemented by three posies of *Paeonia* in white vases arranged along a white marble fireplace.

Plant material: *Paeonia lactiflora* 'Sarah Bernhardt'

Vases: H 15 cm, OP 10 cm

LEFT The round form of the sunflowers (*Helianthus*) is complemented by the tall, linear foxtail lilies (*Eremurus*) and the ring of leaves from the Swiss cheese plant (*Monstera*), which encircles the rim of the tall, straight-sided vase.

Plant material: *Eremurus stenophyllus* and *Helianthus annuus* with *Monstera deliciosa*

Vase: H 40 cm, OP 15 cm

RIGHT A delightful textured design for summer by Bo Büll of Denmark. He has extended the line of the vase with a multitude of slender stems of grasses and wild flowers, marrying the two perfectly with colour and texture through the simple but effective choice of the perfect container.

Plant material: *Allium atropurpureum, Centaurea, Consolida ajacis, Delphinium elatum, Echinops ritro, Sanguisorba officinalis* and *Trifolium pratense* with *Achnatherum splendens*

Vase: H 35 cm, OP 24 cm

ABOVE The contemporary mood of the wallpaper calls for a modern display of flowers and that is what's shown in this mix of vases filled with *Hydrangea* and Guernsey lilies (*Nerine*).

Plant material: *Hydrangea* and *Nerine bowdenii* 'Favoriet'

Vases: Various

RIGHT A robust green container with two decorative side handles is filled with *Dahlia*, sweet William (*Dianthus barbatus*) and *Veronica*.

Plant material: *Dahlia* 'Onesta', *Dianthus barbatus* and *Veronica* 'Smart Iselle'

Vase: H 30 cm, OP 14 cm

ABOVE Stocks (*Matthiola*) are a perennial garden favourite which can now be purchased from the florist all year round, although they are at their best in the summer months. Their tall, linear form suits the straight sides of the tin pail.

Plant material: *Matthiola incana* 'Milka'

Vase: H 24 cm, OP 15 cm

RIGHT *Panicum* 'Fountain' is a lovely floaty grass that is almost ethereal. Here it is combined with light sprays of baby's breath (*Gypsophila*) in one vase with three separate openings.

Plant material: *Gypsophila* with *Panicum* 'Fountain'

Vase: H 12 cm (maximum), OP 20 cm (in total)

ABOVE Not strictly flowers in a vase but it gives that impression! Here Stephen Crisp has placed a plant of winter cherry (*Solanum*) in an exquisite planter and surrounded the rim with wired fir cones and bundles of dried orange slices.

Plant material: *Solanum capsicastrum* with fir cones and *Citrus x sinensis*

Vase: H 25 cm, OP 20 cm

RIGHT All the warmth and colour of autumn are on display here, using garden plant material in a china container (also trying to be a pumpkin). A kebab stick has been placed in the base of each of the mini pumpkins and added to the flowers to give extra texture, colour and even a be talking point.

Plant material: *Calendula officinalis, Ceratostigma* and *Melissa officinalis* with *Cucurbita, Heuchera* 'Blondie in Lime' (Little Cutie Series), *Mentha* and *Hylotelephium* syn. *Sedum spectabile*

Vase: H 11 cm, OP 10 cm

ABOVE The smoke bush (*Cotinus*) is only available commercially for a few months in the autumn but for longer in the garden. The deep rich burgundy colour is wonderful combined with the bright jewel-coloured flowers, fruits and berries available at this time of year.

Plant material: *Rosa* 'Naranja' with *Cotinus coggygria* 'Royal Purple', *Physalis franchetii* and *Rosa* hips

Vase: H 8.5 cm, OP 18 cm

RIGHT In this design, by Annick Mertens at Alden Biesen, lengths of bark surround an inner container filled with autumnal flowers, berries and seed heads.

Plant material: *Dahlia* 'Black Jack', *Dahlia* 'Bonesta', *Dahlia* 'Orange Fox' and *Dahlia* 'Red Cap' with *Clematis* seed heads and *Viburnum opulus* 'Compactum'

Vase: H 20 cm, OP 13 cm

Winter flowers

- The berries of fruiting ivy (*Hedera helix* 'Arborescens'), holly (*Ilex*), St John's wort (*Hypericum*) and *Skimmia* are available at this time of year. They are lovely on their own or with other seasonal plant material. To make the berries even glossier spray them with leaf shine.

- Baubles added to any vase arrangement can make it look festive. To incorporate them in your arrangement remove the claw for hanging and insert a length of strong stem of an appropriate width into the opening. Alternatively insert a barbecue/kebab stick and secure with hot glue.

- Fir cones around the rim of a vase always look effective at this time of year. If they are wired the 'stems' can be inserted inside the container.

- If purchasing a Christmas tree select one that has low branches. Cut these off and use in vase designs. Your tree will never miss them!

- Fresh cranberries can be threaded onto bear grass (*Xerophyllum*) or flexi-grass (*Schoenus*) or decorative wire and looped over flowers to give enclosed space and a larger design. Alternatively, simply float them in water – they will last there for several weeks.

- Candles are a popular feature in Christmas floral designs. In conjunction with a vase it is perhaps best to use a plastic bowl filled with foam that will fit securely in the top. To keep the candles secure, place lengths of kebab sticks on adhesive tape close to the bottom of the candle and impale them in the foam. Ensure that you do not leave a lit candle unattended.

RIGHT This vase, created from lengths of paper glued together, cannot hold water but it is easy to place a glass or jam jar inside. Festive baubles and berries give decoration to one side over the rim. Height is provided on the right with a vertical placement of *Cordyline* bound with decorative twine, with a column of mini *Gerbera* threaded through.

Plant material: mini *Gerbera* 'Black Night' with *Cordyline fruticosa* 'Red Edge'

Vase: H 22 cm, OP 12 cm

LEFT Tall amaryllis (*Hippeastrum*) and glittered gold twigs are arranged in a tall, cylindrical glass vase. The flowers will last for a couple of weeks if purchased in bud but the ends of the stems curl back and look unattractive after a short time. Here a sheet of bark has been wrapped round the base of the vase to give decorative interest and also hide any potential stem curling!

Plant material: *Hippeastrum* (Galaxy Group) 'Red Lion' with *Betula* and bark

Vase: H 40 cm, OP 15 cm

RIGHT St John's wort (*Hypericum*), *Rosa* and the winter-flowering laurustinus (*Viburnum tinus*) are threaded through a mesh of *Cordyline* stems in one of my favourite vases. This vase has the perfect height of 20 cm, with a flared top that lends itself brilliantly to a mass of flowers and foliage.

Plant material: *Rosa* 'Grand Prix' and *Viburnum tinus* with *Cordyline fruticosa* 'Compacta' and *Hypericum* 'Coco Rio'

Vase: H 20 cm, OP 15 cm

Flowers by season

PREVIOUS PAGE Two textured glass cubes hold amaryllis (*Hippeastrum*) cut short, with their stem ends directly in shallow water. Bloom *Chrysanthemum* 'Anastasia' and mini red *Gerbera* are set against the rich foliage of blue spruce (*Picea pungens*) and *Magnolia* leaves. Stephen Crisp has positioned his design on the dining table in the sumptuous setting of Winfield House.

Plant material: *Chrysanthemum* 'Anastasia', mini *Gerbera* 'Wakita' and *Hippeastrum* (Galaxy Group) 'Red Lion' with *Magnolia grandiflora*, *Picea pungens*, *Skimmia japonica*, dried *Malus domestica* and artificial berries

Vases: H 15cm, OP 15 cm

RIGHT An empty candleholder provides the vase for this conical Christmas tree created from a brick of foam trimmed to shape. Short sprigs of box (*Buxus*) cover the wet foam and heads of spray *Rosa* and spray *Chrysanthemum* provide detail. A chain of St John's wort (*Hypericum*) berries threaded on aluminium wire encircles the design.

Plant material: spray *Chrysanthemum* 'Green Lizard' and spray *Rosa* 'Babe' with *Buxus sempervirens* and *Hypericum androsaemum* 'Fire Flair'

Vase: H 10 cm, OP 8 cm

BELOW A Christmas bauble is the perfect mini vase but only when the base is stable. Here baubles, their tops removed with pliers, are perfectly balanced on ceramic yoghurt pots. I have linked the colour of the spray *Rosa* and the mini *Gerbera* to the pots and baubles and placed them on a copper tray with a central candle surrounded by cinnamon sticks on double-sided tape.

Plant material: *Gerbera* 'Wakita' and spray *Rosa* 'Babe'

Vases: H 7 cm, OP 6 cm

ABOVE Blue spruce (*Picea pungens*) has been inserted through chicken wire into a grey urn, followed by *Rosa* 'Grand Prix', spray *Rosa* 'Babe' and St John's wort (*Hypericum*) and finished with wired orange slices. By bringing the chicken wire slightly over the rim of the container it is easier to angle the stems as required.

Plant material: *Leucadendron* 'Safari Sunset', spray *Rosa* 'Babe' and *Rosa* 'Grand Prix' with *Hedera helix* 'Arborescens', *Hypericum* 'Coco Diablo', *Picea pungens*, apples, fir cones and wired *Citrus x sinensis*

Vase: H 18 cm, OP 11 cm

RIGHT One of my favourite colour schemes at Christmas is turquoise, silver and white. This straight-sided turquoise vase was perfect for silver twigs, with long-lasting carnations (*Dianthus*) around the rim. The wires on the small silver baubles and turquoise stars are wrapped around the twigs to keep them in place.

Plant material: *Dianthus* 'Everest' with *Betula*

Vase: H 17 cm, OP 12 cm

LEFT A quick and easy flowering Christmas tree using mini glass tubes to hold the individual heads of three stems of spray *Chrysanthemum* attached with cable ties to stems of gold-sprayed birch (*Betula*) in a tall, heavy vase.

Plant material: spray *Chrysanthemum* 'Anastasia Yellow' with *Betula* and pine (*Pinus*) cones

Vase: H 50 cm, OP 15 cm

ABOVE Branches of *Pinus* are difficult to tame and a loose, relatively unstructured look is the easiest to capture. This green glass vase blends with the different greens of the plant material, which are complemented by a few red roses.

Plant material: *Bupleurum* and *Rosa* 'Grand Prix' with *Asparagus setaceus*, *Hedera helix* 'Arborescens', *Hypericum* 'Coco Rio' and *Pinus sylvestris*

Vase: H 22 cm, OP 15 cm

All year round

- Although many flowers are available 12 months of the year, their quality and longevity may not be as good out of their main growing season.

- *Lilium* open when they are ready and warm rooms, the wafting of a hairdryer, hot water and wishful thinking have little or no effect. If you wish to have open flowers, purchase in bud five days earlier than needed during the summer and seven days earlier in the winter.

- Carnations (*Dianthus*), both spray and bloom, are much underrated. They come in a vast array of colours. The stems don't have the same beauty as their flowers, so disguise these by adding foliage such as hard ruscus (*Ruscus hypophyllum*) or rosemary (*Rosmarinus*), or by cutting them short. If you are lucky to have a mass, simply cut the stems at the front lower.

- Orchids always look exciting and exotic; what's more, they last well. They bloom along a heavy stem, so you will probably need to remove the lower flowers when arranging. Why not place these cut flower heads on short stems in orchid tubes and tuck them in a low bowl among a mass of leaves, such as manipulated *Aspidistra*?

- *Gerbera* and their smaller relations mini *Gerbera* come in a wide range of colours. This cheerful flower is available at most outlets, but check that the petals are intact and there is space around the stems so the heads are not too close to each other.

- Calla (*Zantedeschia*) and *Anthurium* have sculptured forms and attractive smooth green stems that can be incorporated into a vase design. They are both available in lots of different colours.

- The *Vanda* orchid is now grown in a wide range of colours. However, it is the vibrant blue/purple of *Vanda* 'Blue Magic' that is so dramatic and most widely purchased.

- Both bloom and spray *Chrysanthemum* are available all year round. As with carnations (*Dianthus*), use with foliage or flowers that hide the stems and they will reward you with longevity and a light fragrance if the water is kept clean.

- *Rosa* is perhaps the world's favourite flower and comes in many colours. It can be used in virtually any vase arrangement.

RIGHT The ubiquitous carnation (*Dianthus*) often gets a bad press, despite its many redeeming features. It can be purchased in any number of colours and here in the sunlight, in an iridescent glass vase, the mix of hues of both spray and standard flowers will give pleasure for a long time. The stems can look rather stark and knobbly, so cutting them to different lengths will make the viewer more aware that carnations really are very attractive flowers!

Plant material: *Dianthus* 'Prado' (green), *Dianthus* 'Antiqua' (green/peach) and spray *Dianthus* (mixed)

Vase: H 29 cm, OP 20 cm

RIGHT The wonderful bold standard *Chrysanthemum* is available all year round, with colours to suit every season. Here they are arranged with the delicate yellow *Oncidium sphacelatum* 'Golden Shower' orchid. A swirl of lily grass (*Liriope*) gives movement to the design, providing a good contrast to the stiff stems of the *Chrysanthemum*.

Plant material: *Chrysanthemum* 'Anastasia Sunny' and *Oncidium sphacelatum* 'Golden Shower' with *Liriope gigantea*

Vase: H 28 cm, OP 8 cm

ABOVE Mini *Gerbera* are combined with Billy buttons (*Craspedia*) of a similar hue, with a ring of *Galax* leaves which help support the flower stems.

Plant material: *Craspedia globosa* and mini *Gerbera* 'Terra Snooki' with *Galax urceolata*

Vase: H 18 cm, OP 13 cm

LEFT Here a tall glass cylinder has been filled with coils of aluminium wire through which stems of magnificent *Vanda coerulea* 'Blue Magic' orchids were threaded. A few individual flowers were glued to the vase to give added interest and link inside and outside. The unusual colours of *Vanda* and their ability to thrive under water make it an ideal choice for this design.

Plant material: *Vanda coerulea* 'Blue Magic'

Vase: H 60 cm, OP 15 cm

RIGHT A glass cube vase holds a square of floral foam wrapped in a *Cordyline* leaf. An outline of hard ruscus (*Ruscus hypophyllum*) was established first, with the individual *Cymbidium* heads, their stem ends in plastic orchid tubes, then added. Green sweet William (*Dianthus barbatus* 'Green Trick') was then placed in the foam and the whole design enveloped in swirls of flexi-grass (*Schoenus*).

Plant material: *Cymbidium* and *Dianthus barbatus* 'Green Trick' with *Cordyline fruticosa, Ruscus hypophyllum* and *Schoenus melanostachys*

Vase: H 12 cm, OP 12 cm

ABOVE Sales of roses exceed those of all other flowers. Loved in every corner of the world, roses look delightful arranged with other flowers or simply on their own, as in this massed design in a fluted round vase.

Plant material: *Rosa* 'Ocean Song' and *Rosa* 'Sweet Avalanche'

Vase: H 17 cm, OP 11 cm

RIGHT *Lilium* is the perfect flower to purchase in bud and allow to develop without fuss or bother over two weeks, whatever month of the year. Take care when arranging at home that you do not place the lilies too close to wallpaper or fabric as the pollen from the stamens does stain. Remove the pollen gently with a tissue rather than scissors to avoid an unattractive cut. Note that all parts of *Lilium* are extremely poisonous to cats.

Plant material: *Lilium* 'Pontiac'

Vase: H 32 cm, OP 7 cm

LEFT Stems of *Anthurium* have been bound with thin wire at regular intervals to *Phormium* leaves with their soft tips removed. A further *Phormium* leaf has been swirled round the base of each cylinder vase to give additional interest.

Plant material: *Anthurium andreanum* 'Pistache' with *Phormium tenax*

Vases: left H 60 cm, OP 15 cm; middle H 80 cm, OP 15 cm; right H 40 cm, OP 15 cm

RIGHT Singapore/Thai/Florida orchids (*Dendrobium*) have a linear form and are available all year round. I love their clean lines in a simple uncomplicated vase. Remove any blooms that would lie below the rim.

Plant material: *Dendrobium* 'White Jumbo'

Vase: H 20 cm, OP 7 cm

There are dominant colours for each of the seasons – pink, blue and yellow for spring, a mix of every colour for summer, deep rich tones for autumn and red, gold and white for the winter festive season. So if you do not have seasonal flowers think colour to create the mood.

In all areas of design, fashions change. Often designers look to other countries or to the past and reinvent. For example, hanging designs have long been used in Japanese homes and designs within the vase are reminiscent of the Wardian cases of the Victorian era. However, the concept of balancing stems over the rim of the vase and the incorporation of new materials show that there is always a way forward.

8
Styles and techniques

Structures with mini vases

Tiny glass vases are now available commercially in the shape of test tubes, sea horses, bottles and so on. The base is sometimes rounded, so if they are unable to stand up on their own hang or tie them to structures of stems, such as bamboo (*Bambusa*), dogwood (*Cornus*) or willow (*Salix*). If you cannot find these use the plastic tubes that come with Singapore/ Florida orchids (*Dendrobium*) instead. Wrap them with a leaf, which you can then tie in place with narrow ribbon, wool, raffia, twine, aluminium or decorative reel wire.

RIGHT In this contemporary design a structure of twigs, held together with decorative yellow cable ties, stands in a shallow glass vase. A colourful mix of spring flowers has been slipped through the structure into the water at the base.

Plant material: *Anemone coronaria* and *Ranunculus asiaticus* with *Cornus sericea* 'Flaviramea'

Vase: H 10 cm, OP 15 cm

LEFT Glass tubes tucked inside rolls of bark and secured in a floral ring become mini vases into which orchid heads and preserved oak leaves have been tucked. Lengths of *Phormium* have been pinned round the ring and a length of twine helps secure the leaves in place.

Plant material: *Cymbidium* with *Betula* bark, *Phormium*, *Quercus rubra* (preserved) and *Rosa* hips

Vases: H 8 cm, OP 2 cm

Leaf manipulation

Manipulation means changing a leaf into a different form. Manipulated leaves are great at the base of tall, linear designs of foxgloves (*Digitalis*), foxtail lilies (*Eremurus*) or *Gladiolus*. This can be done by plaiting, rolling, stapling, weaving – any way you want. Here I show how to create some simple but effective manipulation that can be added to your flowers in a vase.

Clipping

If you want to tidy up or reduce the size of large leaves, such as *Fatsia*, simply cut the tips from the leaves and add around the rim of a vase or incorporate in large design work.

Looping

Aspidistra leaves are ideal for looping. Fold the tip down to the point where the leaf meets the stalk. Place a small piece of florist's fix, a glue dot, Plasticine or Blu-tack close to the tip on the inside of the leaf. Press the two parts of the leaf together firmly and you will have created a loop.

Rolling

Galax or *Bergenia* leaves are ideal for rolling. To keep the roll secure, place florist's fix or similar on the outside of the leaf. Alternatively, staple or insert a decorative or dressmaker's pin through the leaf vertically.

RIGHT A mass of *Rosa* 'Grand Prix' and green sweet William (*Dianthus barbatus* 'Green Trick') has a collar of *Aspidistra*. The tips of the leaves have been brought round and under and then been secured to frame the flowers beautifully.

Plant material: *Dianthus barbatus* 'Green Trick' and *Rosa* 'Grand Prix' with *Aspidistra elatior*

Vase: H 14 cm, OP 6 cm

Wiring

Place a heavy-gauge wire along the back of the central rib of an *Aspidistra* or other strong leaf so that one end of the wire stops about 3 cm from the tip, with the other end at the base of the leaf lamina. Cover the wire with preferably wide florist's tape. Make sure that the leaf surface is dry so that the tape does not come unstuck.

BELOW A round vase has been filled with wired and manipulated variegated *Aspidistra* leaves. Lemon mini *Gerbera* provide visual impact.

Plant material: mini *Gerbera* 'Lemon Ice' with *Aspidistra variegata*

Vase: H 20 cm, OP 18 cm

In the vase

Flowers last for a surprisingly long time inside the vase, as a mini greenhouse effect is created. The stems can be kept in place on a pin holder, with lengths of builder's lead wrapped round each individual stem to keep them vertical, or by using scrunched-up decorative aluminium wire through which the stems can be threaded. A network of flexible stems like *Cornus* (dogwood) or *Salix* (willow) can also be used as a mechanic inside the vase.

ABOVE Although contemporary in style, this design harks back to the Wardian case, where growing plants were kept in glass to extend their lives. Here parrot *Tulipa* have been threaded through aluminium wire with their stem ends in water.

Plant material: *Tulipa* 'Apricot'

Vase: H 23 cm, OP 18 cm

LEFT A pin holder at the base of the vase secures three roses at different heights. A length of dogwood (*Cornus*) is coiled round the base, with a topping of moss to hide the mechanics.

Plant material: *Rosa* 'Grand Prix' with *Cornus alba* 'Sibirica' and *Plagiothecium*

Vase: H 28 cm, OP 13 cm

RIGHT The opening of a tall cylinder vase holds a low bowl filled with foam. *Phalaenopsis* orchids tumble down and mitsumata sticks rise upwards. A swirl of grass gives interest inside the vase. *Sempervivum* and *Rosa* form the dominant area at the centre of the design.

Plant material: *Phalaenopsis* 'Monte Carlo' and *Rosa* 'Tacazzi' with *Edgeworthia*, *Schoenus melanostacys* and *Sempervivum*

Vase: H 60 cm, OP 15 cm

RIGHT This contemporary design uses the inside and the outside of the vase to great effect. Two branches have been balanced over the rim of the glass cylinder vase to heighten interest and add volume to the design. *Phormium* leaves and calla (*Zantedeschia*) have been placed vertically and trails of *Amaranthus* flow downwards.

Plant material: *Amaranthus caudatus* and *Zantedeschia* 'Captain Samba' with *Fatsia japonica*, *Parthenocissus tricuspidata* and *Phormium tenax*

Vase: H 40 cm, OP 15 cm

Around the vase

This is not the most obvious way of using a vase, but to create an unusual contemporary effect place twigs or long-lasting leaves around the vase secured under a rubber band and hidden with a decorative wrap of aluminium wire or wool.

RIGHT An arrangement of *Gladiolus* and a single stem of *Hydrangea* in a tall cylinder vase is made more exciting by the vertical placement of bleached white mitsumata sticks around the vase, bound on with wire.

Plant material: *Gladiolus* 'Milka' and *Hydrangea* with *Edgeworthia* and *Panicum* 'Fountain'

Vase: H 40 cm, OP 15 cm

Multiple placements

Simple arrangements can become very powerful when several are used together, perhaps in a row or a circle. Fruits, petals or night lights can be interspersed between the placements to give additional interest.

ABOVE Every home has a narrow ledge or shelf which lends itself perfectly to the placement of a line of small vases. Here, the 'odd one out' works thanks to its position off centre to give interesting contrast. If it had been placed at either end of the row of four there would have been too much dominance to one side and the overall design would not have appeared balanced.

Plant material: *Muscari armeniacum* and *Ranunculus asiaticus*

Vases: H 11 cm, OP 5 cm (three vases); H 11 cm, OP 4 cm (single vase)

ABOVE This kitchen window ledge is just wide enough to take a line of small vases, each containing a few flowers from the late summer garden.

Plant material: *Hydrangea, Leucanthemum vulgare, Lobelia* and *Rosa* with *Symphoricarpos albus*

Vases: Various

ABOVE These purple vases create a graceful duo with the purple throat of the white *Cymbidium* orchid giving a harmonious link. The cluster of carnations (*Dianthus*) and green sweet William (*Dianthus barbatus* 'Green Trick'), surrounded by a ring of *Galax* leaves in the vase to the fore, creates both contrast and harmony.

Plant material: *Cymbidium*, *Dianthus barbatus* 'Green Trick' and *Dianthus* 'Belle Epoque' with *Aspidistra elatior*, *Fatsia japonica*, *Galax urceolata* and *Schoenus melanostachys*

Vases: tallest H 24 cm, OP 6 cm; shortest H 20 cm, OP 9 cm

Vintage

Vintage means recreating the feel and mood of bygone years using flowers and vases reminiscent of that period. The 1930s, 1940s and 1950s have been very popular in recent years and teacups and saucers make the perfect vase. Old tea sets are often broken up and odd items are very inexpensive and easy to find in charity shops.

RIGHT An earthenware jug purchased from a car boot sale holds *Hyacinthus* blooms placed in a minimalist fashion.

Plant material: *Hyacinthus orientalis* 'China Pink'

Vase: H 18 cm, OP 13 cm

RIGHT Vintage is a trend that many enjoy, but some vases from the 1930s are not easy to fill as they are wide with sloping sides. It is best to keep stems short and to make sure you have enough of them!

Plant material: *Cymbidium* 'Red Star' and *Rosa* 'Bombastic' with *Aeonium decorum, Aeonium* 'Poldark', *Ajuga reptans* 'Black Scallop', *Ceropegia linearis* subsp. *woodii, Echeveria* 'Black Prince', *Erica tetralix* 'Rosea', *Heuchera* 'Amethyst Myst', *Heuchera* 'Autumn Haze', *Leucothoe keiskei* 'Burning Love', *Ophiopogon planiscapus* 'Nigrescens', *Rhipsalis baccifera* syn. *R. cassutha* and *Sempervivum* 'Gamma'

Vase: H 14 cm, OP 28 cm

ABOVE Two elegant antique glass vases standing on the window ledge in a drawing room hold a mix of white and pastel flowers which harmonise well with the clarity of the glass.

Plant material: *Astrantia* 'Superstar', *Phlox paniculata* 'Ice Cap' and *Rosa* 'Crème de la Crème'

Vases: H 10 cm, OP 5 cm

Parallel style

Letter-box vases, with narrow rectangular openings, lend themselves to parallel or landscape designs. This style simply means that the flowers and foliage are arranged vertically in the container and the mechanic is usually foam, which enables more precise positioning of the stems.

RIGHT *Hyacinthus* stores energy in the bulbous white ends of its stem and is quite happy to be out of water as the flowers blossom. This feature is used to advantage in this contemporary design where twigs, secured in foam, rise out of the vase and are threaded horizontally with the flowers. The height of the twigs is greater than in classic proportions because of the space between the twigs, which gives a light, ethereal quality.

Plant material: *Hyacinthus orientalis* with *Betula pubescens*

Vase: H 15 cm, OP 17 cm

Hanging

LEFT This unusual blue rubber vase from IKEA calls out for special treatment. A sliver of foam is wedged at the base to support staggered vertical placements of Guernsey lilies (*Nerine*). A line of long-lasting ice plants (*Hylotelephium* syn. *Sedum spectabile*) encircles the circumference of the rim, with one stem filling the hole top centre.

Plant material: *Nerine bowdenii* 'Favoriet' and *Hylotelephium* syn. *Sedum spectabile*

Vase: H 20 cm, OP 32 cm

Wall vases have long been popular in Japan, where space in the home is at a premium. In the 1920s and 1930s in the UK there was a vogue for wall sconces and I think this one warrants a revival. As the Japanese realised, beauty can be observed at eye level when every centimetre of floor space is taken.

ABOVE This shiny turquoise vintage wall vase, packed with chicken wire, holds a mix of flowers and foliage on short stems which follow the shape of the vase.

Plant material: *Alchemilla mollis*, *Alstroemeria* 'Siberia' and *Matthiola incana* with *Heuchera villosa* 'Palace Purple'

Vase: H 12 cm, OP 20 cm

Massing/grouping/blocking

In classic work the plant material is generally scattered through the design, but massing, grouping or blocking (all three words describe the same technique) the flowers and foliage means the opposite. Numbers of flowers of the same variety are placed together to give a more contemporary feel. The types of flowers and/or foliage used are usually limited. Good balance is harder to achieve but the look can be stunning. The vase needs to be bold and strong, preferably with a non-patterned finish. It can be variously textured to link with the plant material used in the design.

RIGHT Tall stems of giant onion (*Allium giganteum*) have been massed in a tin vase with *Aspidistra* leaves threaded through so the stems are hidden. The lengths of stem not used have been inserted separately to give an interesting decorative detail. The raffia-covered baked bean tins to the side hold *Heuchera* leaves in a toning colour.

Plant material: *Allium giganteum* with *Aspidistra elatior* and *Heuchera villosa* 'Palace Purple'

Vases: tallest H 34 cm, OP 14 cm; shortest H 10.5 cm, OP 3.5 cm

ABOVE *Pinus* is one of my favourite evergreen foliages. There are different pines available – long and short, smooth and hard. *Pinus strobus* is brilliant. Its spiky texture offers total contrast to the smooth surface of the vase. The original intention was to add orchids but I just loved it as is, massed with no embellishment and no added colour. Simple beauty in its own right.

Plant material: *Pinus strobus*

Vase: H 31 cm, OP 8 cm

ABOVE Grape hyacinths (*Muscari*) have been massed to one side to be in scale with the single rose that is placed low in the design.

Plant material: *Muscari armeniacum* and *Rosa* 'Wham'

Vase: H 8 cm, OP 16 cm

RIGHT A small opening in a tall vase has been used to great effect by taking a mass of long lengths of steel grass (*Xanthorrhoea australis*) and tucking the ends under a tight band of raffia, thus creating a cage that encloses both space and the vase.

Plant material: *Viburnum opulus* 'Roseum' with *Xanthorrhoea australis*

Vase: H 41 cm, OP 2 cm

There will always be new approaches to styles and techniques, but using the information given in this book you will never find them difficult to follow.

Unusual vases are often inherited, or gifts, or school and church bazaar purchases, or even dismal mistakes, but do try to love them all, as you can create some exciting original designs using them. Here are a few pointers to the easiest ones to use – and maybe those to avoid too!

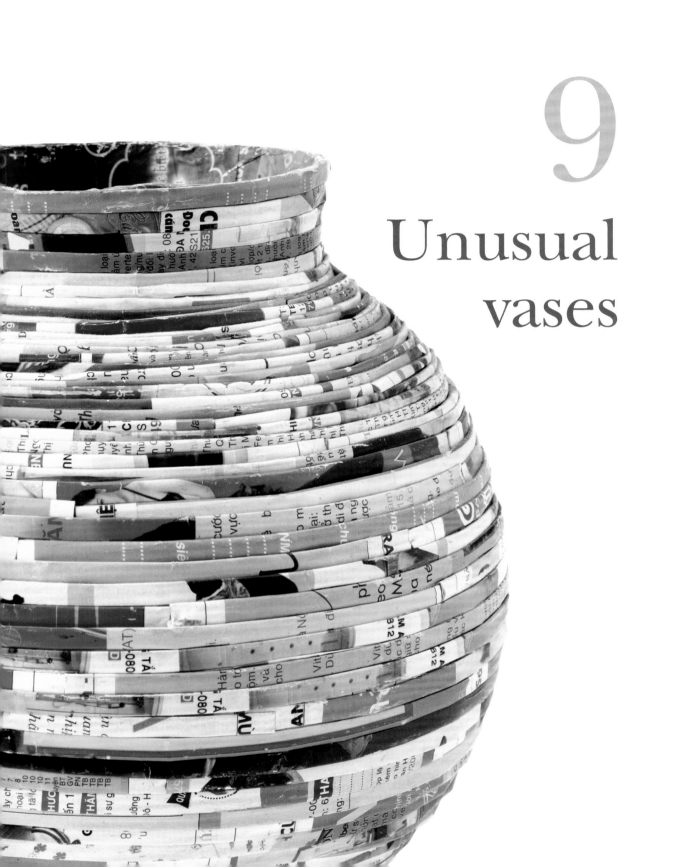

9

Unusual vases

Key points and tips

- Vases more than 30 cm high are difficult to fill effectively and you will need to choose flowers that are at least 60 cm tall.

- Symmetric vases are usually easier to work with than those that are asymmetrical.

- Hollow polystyrene hemispheres are available online and they can be decorated in many ways. Try pinning on long-lasting leaves such as hard ruscus (*Ruscus hypophyllum*), *Eucalyptus* or squares of *Aspidistra* leaves to create an interesting vase into which an inexpensive waterproof inner container can be slipped. You could also stick these on with cold glue.

- If you like the idea of purchasing 'difficult' unusual vases try T.K. Maxx for one-off creations or visit car boot or jumble sales and charity shops.

- IKEA is a huge international company and their range of vases, though not huge, is always good value and sometimes there are interesting bargains to pick up. Pound shops also have great buys if you visit regularly.

- When checking out charity shops, I think the best buys are to be had in upmarket towns or places where people go to retire and want to downsize.

- Think out of the box and consider items such as beer bottles, yoghurt pots, ramekins and coffee cups as vases.

RIGHT The leaves of hard ruscus (*Ruscus hypophyllum*) have been pinned to a polystyrene hemisphere. The 'vase' was then tightly packed with a mix of colourful flowers enlivened by the addition of green sweet William (*Dianthus barbatus* 'Green Trick').

Plant material: *Delphinium, Dianthus barbatus* 'Green Trick', *Eustoma russellianum* 'Rosita Blue', *Ranunculus asiaticus* 'Elegance Cerise Pink', spray *Rosa* 'Mirabel', *Rosa* 'Red Naomi' and *Viola* with *Ruscus hypophyllum*

Vase: H 12.5 cm, OP 25 cm

Unusual vases

ABOVE I saw this design by Lucy Allan in two yellow Hunter wellington boots in the parish church in Byley, Cheshire, and loved it. They provide the perfect 'vases' for daffodils (*Narcissus*) and stems of pussy willow (*Salix*) for Easter.

Plant material: *Narcissus* 'King Alfred' and *Salix caprea*

Vases: H 19 cm, OP 10 cm

RIGHT In a contemporary living area Philipp von Arx has used ostrich and goose eggs, supported on wire stands, to create innovative vases for yellow *Narcissus* 'Tête-à-Tête', which add a splash of colour to the room.

Plant material: *Narcissus* 'Tête-à-Tête'

Vases: largest H 15 cm, OP 4 cm; smallest H 7 cm, OP 3 cm

LEFT Five Kronenbourg beer bottles make the perfect vases for nodding yellow nasturtiums (*Tropaeolum*) picked from the garden. This wonderful flower self-seeds each year, so a packet is a good investment. Their asymmetric, volumetric form shows to best advantage when not mixed with other flowers. A few sprigs of mint have been added for their long-lasting quality and wonderful fragrance.

Plant material: *Tropaeolum majus* with *Mentha*

Vases: H 18 cm, OP 2.5 cm

RIGHT The opening of this Art Deco vase is minute, but the stiff, slender stem of the yarrow (*Achillea*) and a garden fern slipped in easily and reinforced the 1930s feel. Both the yarrow and fern will dry in situ to make a long-lasting design.

Plant material: *Achillea filipendulina* with *Dryopteris*

Vase: H 18 cm, OP 1 cm

BELOW Dynamic but simple: this bold and contemporary design by Philipp von Arx uses light-bulb glass vases to hold single stems of Guernsey lilies (*Nerine*). The addition of a base means these vases stay upright.

Plant material: *Nerine bowdenii* 'Vesta'

Vases: H 12 cm, OP 2 cm

LEFT In this design by Burnley and Whalley & District Flower Clubs at Towneley Hall bottles of all shapes and sizes have been wrapped in wool of different colours and textures to provide decorative vases for sunflowers (*Helianthus*) and other flowers.

Plant material: *Anthurium, Chrysanthemum* 'Anastasia', *Delphinium, Dendrobium* 'Sonia' (dyed), mini *Gerbera* 'Petticoat' and *Helianthus annuus*

Vases: Various

RIGHT A strip of artificial grass has been wrapped round a square glass vase to which double-sided tape has been attached. Different carnations (*Dianthus*) fill the vase. I love the way the artificial grass mimics the colour and texture of the living green sweet William (*Dianthus barbatus* 'Green Trick'). The purple throats of the *Phalaenopsis* give a colour link and create exciting contrast. Coloured aluminium wire links the whole.

Plant material: *Dianthus barbatus* 'Green Trick', *Dianthus* 'Dark Farida' and *Phalaenopsis* 'Omega'

Vase: H 15 cm, OP 15 cm

The vases shown in this book are just a tiny selection of what is available. Anything that has an opening and will hold water can be termed a vase, so use your imagination and find those that will inspire your creativity and bring excitement and originality to your home.

Having worked with flowers for many years and taught thousands of students, I would love to be able to say that colour or fragrance ranks first when people choose flowers. However, the prime quality that usually comes to their mind is longevity. That said, it is possible to have beauty and style in long-lasting designs. This is how you do it.

BELOW Medicine bottles may be small but a collection can create a large display. By using repetition, either in colour or in the choice of plant material, the larger design will come together effortlessly. Here yarrow (*Achillea*) is teamed with *Pittosporum* and some garden ferns. The yarrow will dry in situ and retain its colour, so you will need to replace only the foliage.

Plant material: *Achillea filipendulina* with *Pittosporum tobira* and ferns including *Nephrolepis* and *Adiantum*

Vases: tallest H 17 cm, OP 2 cm; shortest H 9 cm, OP 2 cm

Long-lasting arrangements

RIGHT Dried *Lavandula* has been used to decorate a damaged cube vase by tucking stems under a rubber band covered with wool. *Sempervivum* plants have been placed in the centre of the cube. They are happy with very little care and will last and last without watering.

Plant material: *Lavandula angustifolia* with *Sempervivum*

Vase: H 10 cm, OP 10 cm

ABOVE Chincherinchee/star of Bethlehem (*Ornithogalum*) is one of the longest-lasting flowers. If purchased in bud they can last for three weeks or more. For this design, the flowers were left out of water prior to arranging so the stems became more flexible. They were then curved gently in the hands and inserted into a low glass vase together with a bunch of flexi-grass (*Schoenus*).

Plant material: *Ornithogalum arabicum* with *Schoenus melanostachys*

Vase: H 15 cm, OP 20 cm

Long-lasting arrangements

BELOW AND RIGHT Two designs in the same vase, both incorporating vibrant variegated holly (*Ilex*) and fruiting ivy (*Hedera helix* 'Arborescens') with its luscious black berries. In the design on the right, red *Skimmia* berries add further interest and below a few gold-sprayed twigs create a trouble-free design. Both will last for weeks. The Constance Spry urn-shaped vase is fabulous, but its wide opening requires a lot of plant material. However, using easily acquired foliage from the garden or hedgerow makes this a large but inexpensive design.

Plant material: *Hedera helix* 'Arborescens' and *Ilex* x *altaclerensis* 'Golden King', *Skimmia japonica* with *Betula*

Vase: H 18 cm, OP 15 cm

ABOVE Drawing rooms are often the least-used room in the house, so a vase of dried or other long-lasting flowers would be ideal, especially if time is at a premium. This unusual vase has an incredibly small opening in relation to its overall size, but the long, slim stems of larch (*Larix*) slipped easily inside. For the wow factor I added sprigs of dried *Hydrangea*, sprayed with a light dusting of gold, around the rim to create a soft collar of plant material.

Plant material: *Hydrangea* with *Larix decidua*

Vase: H 32 cm, OP 4 cm

RIGHT Vintage faux flowers have muted colours and give the impression of having been gently dried. This round vase with subdued colouring repeats the shape of the flowers beautifully and reflects the mood.

Plant material: *Hydrangea, Papaver, Rosa* and *Tulipa* with *Eucalyptus*

Vase: H 14 cm, OP 10 cm

RIGHT A blue glazed vase holds a mix of beautiful silk flowers in pinks, creams and lime green.

Plant material: *Paeonia, Rosa* and *Viburnum opulus* 'Roseum' (silk flowers)

Vase: H 17 cm, OP 43 cm

LEFT Dried yarrow (*Achillea*), *Eucalyptus* and *Hydrangea* have been arranged in a lemon-yellow vase. These flowers are easy to buy or to cut from the garden and they all dry well when mature. The arrangement has been positioned against fabric that reflects the soft, muted colours of the flowers.

Plant material: *Achillea filipendulina* and *Hydrangea* with *Eucalyptus cinerea*

Vase: H 23 cm, OP 12 cm

RIGHT Succulents are extremely popular at the moment. They are easy to propagate, stylish and long-lasting. Here, a number of them have been grouped on a bed of moss, together with small pieces of slate, in a low glass vase. They will remain happy and trouble-free like this for many weeks, if not months.

Plant material: *Echeveria* (various), *Sempervivum* and *Pachyphytum*

Vase: H 12 cm, OP 18 cm

I hope this book will give you ideas and inspiration to fill any vase you have at home. And if you have a vase that defies all the tips and techniques given just email me – you never know, if there is ever a Volume 2, it may be included!

The Judith Blacklock Flower School

After reading this book you may wish to come and experience for yourself how to arrange flowers at Judith's delightful school in a flower-filled mews in the heart of Knightsbridge, London.

The school offers a wide range of courses covering almost every aspect of flowers, both as a hobby and as a profession.

Established for 16 years, it is widely acclaimed as the UK's foremost flower school. Judith is renowned worldwide for her ability to convey her knowledge to amateur and professional flower designers alike. The highly regarded courses are accredited by the British Accreditation Council (BAC) and the American Institute of Floral Designers (AIFD). There are timetables to suit all schedules and levels and online courses.

At the school, we teach in a logical, straightforward way that really does work. Once you know the techniques, we encourage you to develop your own individual style based on structured guidelines. We believe that everybody can succeed and our students prove that this

is so – many now run successful flower companies or simply enjoy arranging flowers for themselves more confidently.

On longer courses we have an exceptional team of tutors who have their own particular expertise – they are both professional florists and experienced qualified tutors. Judith teaches on nearly every course, so that she can understand the aims and objectives of every student and help wherever she can.

Acknowledgements

I have loved writing and designing for *Arranging Flowers in a Vase*. I can do the basics with some ease, thanks to my many years of experience, but it is only with the help of a team of trusted colleagues and friends, dedicated professionals all, that this book has finally come to print in its present form.

Julia Harker at the Flower School has been meticulous in her attention to detail and has worked wonders with the organisation of images and content.

Amanda Hawkes, without whom I simply could not create, has designed another book for me which charms through its inventive but disciplined format. I am convinced that her designs help to make learning easy – which is always my objective.

Lesley Levene and Dr Christina Curtis have laboured away to ensure that the text is clear and the botanical nomenclature is accurate. Both have extraordinary skills and I would be lost without them.

Once I decided that I wanted to include coloured illustrations, there was only one person to ask. Tomoko Takamoto has an extraordinary gift for turning my rough sketches into charming drawings that inform as well as looking wonderful on the page.

My photographers have been marvellous and I have enjoyed working with all of them. Although I created most of the designs in this book, I was lucky to have had the assistance of tutors at the Flower School, Bo Büll, Stephen Crisp, Mo Duffill, Philipp von Arx, Marco Wamelink and of course my lead technician, Tomasz Koson, whose hand-tied bouquets are second to none. His help at my Flower School is invaluable.

I am confident that you will both learn and be inspired by *Arranging Flowers in a Vase*. My greatest wish is that it will enable you to approach your arrangements with fresh eyes and be thoroughly delighted by the results.

Photographic credits

Abdulrahman Alyousef: 4

Judith Blacklock: 11, 33, 41, 47, 50, 62, 67, 70, 73, 84, 91, 93, 100, 102, 112, 115, 118, 130, 131 (top), 132, 133, 135, 146, 152, 155, 161, 165, 170, 175, 184, 191, 194, 196, 203, 204, 212–213, 221, 224, 228, 246, 247, 255, 265, 267

Jean-Pierre Bonello: 121, 148, 205

Concept factory: 49, 158

Oliver Gordon: front cover, 17, 19, 22, 24, 26, 28, 29, 30, 31, 37 (right), 38, 39, 44, 51, 53, 54, 55, 56, 57, 63, 65, 66, 68, 71, 80, 81, 86, 88, 96, 97, 99, 101, 107, 108, 109, 110, 111, 116 (top and bottom), 117, 120, 125, 126 (top), 127 (bottom), 128, 129, 131 (bottom), 136, 137, 142, 145, 151, 153, 156, 159, 160, 162–163, 166, 167, 168-169, 171, 173, 174, 177, 178, 179, 182, 183, 185, 186, 187, 189, 190, 193, 195, 200, 206, 208, 209, 218, 220, 222, 223, 229, 236, 237, 240, 241, 242–243, 244, 245, 251, 252-253, 254, 256-257, 258, 259, 260, 261, 262, 263, 266

Alice Hall: 23

Lucy Heath: 13, 37 (left), 46, 48, 60, 119, 127 (top), 197

Thomas de Hoghton: 16, 45, 59, 69, 72, 85, 89, 113, 140, 149, 192, 207, 219, 233, 234 (234 courtesy of *The Flower Arranger*)

Lewis Khan: 64, 74-75, 82, 90, 103, 114, 143, 144, 147, 201, 210-211, 214, 215

Steve Merryfield: 25, 83, 225

Clive Nichols: 52, 172, 180–181

Jeanette Phillipson: 32, 157

Tobias Smith: 79

Mark Weeks: 2-3, 9, 15, 21, 35, 77, 87, 105, 123, 139, 199, 216-217, 227, 231, 249, 270-271

Unknown: 235, 238-239

Other titles from The Flower Press

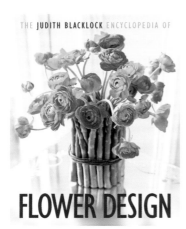

The Judith Blacklock Encyclopedia
of Flower Design
ISBN 978 0 9552391 0 6

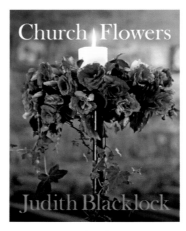

Church
Flowers
ISBN 978 0 9552391 6 8

Flower Arranging
The complete guide for beginners
ISBN 978 0 9552391 7 5

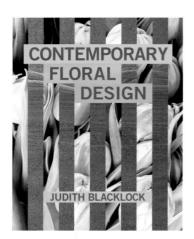

Contemporary
Floral Design
ISBN 978 0 9552391 9 9

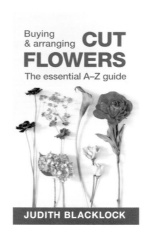

Buying & Arranging Cut Flowers
The essential A–Z guide
ISBN 978 0 9935715 0 3

Floristry
A step-by-step guide
ISBN 978 0 9552391 5 1

TO ORDER
Order these books through any bookshop or online retailer.
In the UK you can order direct from the publisher:
Tel: 01202 586848   www.selectps.com